Student Study and Retrieval Guide for

PSYCHOLOGY IN YOUR LIFE

FOURTH HIGH SCHOOL EDITION

LORI HODIN
Lincoln Sudbury Regional High School

ROB MCENTARFFER
Lincoln Public Schools

W. W. NORTON & COMPANY
Celebrating a Century of Independent Publishing

W. W. Norton & Company has been independent since its founding in 1923, when William Warder Norton and Mary D. Herter Norton first published lectures delivered at the People's Institute, the adult education division of New York City's Cooper Union. The firm soon expanded its program beyond the Institute, publishing books by celebrated academics from America and abroad. By midcentury, the two major pillars of Norton's publishing program—trade books and college texts—were firmly established. In the 1950s, the Norton family transferred control of the company to its employees, and today—with a staff of five hundred and hundreds of trade, college, and professional titles published each year—W. W. Norton & Company stands as the largest and oldest publishing house owned wholly by its employees.

Director of High School Publishing: Jenna Bookin Barry
High School Media Editor: Alicia Jimenez
High School Editorial Assistant: Katelyn Taylor
High School Intern: Madison Fuchs
High School Marketing Manager: AM Anastasi
Project Editor: Christine D'Antonio
Managing Editor, College: Marian Johnson
Managing Editor, College Digital Media: Kim Yi
Production Manager: Richard Bretan
Composition: Westchester Publishing Services
Manufacturing: LCS Communications

ISBN: 978-1-324-04711-7

W. W. Norton & Company, Inc., 500 Fifth Avenue, New York, NY 10110
wwnorton.com
W. W. Norton & Company Ltd., 15 Carlisle Street, London W1D 3BS

ABOUT THE AUTHORS

Lori Hodin

Lincoln Sudbury Regional High School

Lori Hodin teaches psychology and is the coordinator of Safe School Initiatives at Lincoln Sudbury Regional High School in Sudbury, MA. She loves teaching psychology and has worked with high school students and AP psychology teachers for 25 years. As Safe Schools Coordinator, she uses psychology in peer mediation training, violence prevention assemblies, and leadership development. She also uses her psychology background as an assistant coach for the girls' rugby team. She enjoys taking her dogs for walks and visiting with her grown children, friends, and family.

Rob McEntarffer, PhD

Lincoln Public Schools

Rob McEntarffer taught psychology, AP psychology, and philosophy for 13 years at Lincoln Southeast high school in Lincoln, NE, and was involved with the AP psychology reading for many years. While teaching, he became interested in educational measurement issues and got a master's degree in educational measurement (qualitative and quantitative methods) from the University of Nebraska, Lincoln in 2003. Rob started his work as an assessment/evaluation specialist with Lincoln Public Schools in 2005, and works with the district on large-scale and classroom assessment issues. Rob earned his PhD in teaching, learning, and teacher education in 2013, focusing his research on how teachers make room for formative assessment processes in their classrooms. Rob lives with his wife, two kids, dog, and cat in Lincoln and works for Lincoln Public Schools.

CONTENTS

INTRODUCTION

Congratulations! Since you are reading this retrieval guide, you have access to one of the best and most well-researched college-level introductory psychology textbooks in the world: *Psychology in Your Life* by Sarah Grison (psychological researcher and expert in teaching introductory psychology) and Michael Gazzaniga (one of the most famous biopsychology researchers of the modern era of psychology). Since psychology is the science of thinking and behavior, you can expect to learn amazing things from this textbook. It's all about you: how you think and act in the ways you do, how you experience the world, how you influence other people, and how they influence you. Psychology is a fascinating science because everything we learn relates to each of us.

Since you're going to be reading about amazing and potentially important research findings in this textbook, we want to make sure you are able to remember and use what you learn. Much of the research you will read about can help you solve important problems and enrich your life in the future. You've probably heard teachers' advice about textbooks before. When teachers say things like "Make sure you study that chapter in the textbook," what they mean is that there is information in the chapter that you will need later. But what does it mean to "study" a chapter in a textbook? Should you read the chapter once, then re-read it? Take notes about what you read? Highlight important phrases? What's the best way to study a textbook chapter?

Good news! You have another advantage because you are in a psychology class and have this textbook: many psychological researchers have been investigating the best ways to study, and they have some answers. It turns out that there are some ways of studying that are much more effective and take much less time than others. You'll learn details about the cognitive psychology research about this topic in chapter 7 (Memory). One quick way to summarize the research is this: we remember what we think about. That may sound obvious, but that simple idea has major implications for efficient and effective studying. Right now, you are reading what we call the "Retrieval Guide" for your textbook. We call it a *retrieval* guide as well as a *study* guide because it is structured to emphasize one of the most important aspects of your memory system: retrieval! One of the most consistent findings in cognitive psychology is that the more often we retrieve information from our memory system, the stronger that memory becomes "encoded" in our long-term memory, and the more likely it is that we can remember and use it in the future. Your textbook also features many learning strategies (tips, goals, pauses) and application opportunities ("Using Psychology in Your Life") based on this research. As you use this retrieval guide, you'll notice that it asks you to think about what you are reading, rather than just copy information from the textbook. Using this retrieval guide will help you think deeply about what you are reading, retrieve important information, express it in your own words, and prove to yourself that you know it (before you have to know it on a test).

Here's what you'll find in the Retrieval Guide for each chapter:

- **PRE-READING QUESTIONS**: It may feel strange to try to answer questions about the content of the chapter *before* you even read it, but thinking about some of the big issues in the chapter before you learn the research is likely to help you encode the research into your long-term memory. Answer these questions before you read the chapter, then come back to these questions after you're finished reading and evaluate/change your initial answers.

- **RETRIEVE-AS-YOU-GO QUESTIONS**: We wrote questions specifically designed to help you think about what you are reading while you are reading it. This can save you a lot of time: Instead of reading a chapter and then going back to study it, thinking deeply while you read can help you encode that information immediately. After you read each section, try to answer the retrieve-as-you-go questions. Make sure you don't "cheat" while you answer these questions: read the section, then close your book (or the tab in your browser), answer the questions as well as you can, then open the book again and change your answers as needed. This will probably feel like a lot of "pop quizzes" as you read through the chapter, and that's actually a good thing! You are experiencing "retrieval practice" (also called the "testing effect"). You are forcing your memory system to retrieve what you initially learned, and that retrieval or "pop quiz" process will dramatically increase how well you know the information (Dunlosky et al., 2013). (A complete reference list is included in your textbook.)

- **USING PSYCHOLOGY IN YOUR LIFE**: In this section, you will pick one option from the provided choices that resonates with you. Thinking about personal examples and connecting your learning to what is personally relevant enhances recall and understanding and can be useful in your school and social life!

- **KEY TAKEAWAYS**: This section highlights "news you can use" to consolidate your learning and help you think like a psychologist. The more you learn, the more you will see that psychology is everywhere!

- **THE BIG QUESTION**: Each chapter ends with one big question related to an important idea or theme from that chapter. The best way to use big questions is to answer them before you think you are ready to move on to another chapter. If you can answer the big question in your own words using terms from the chapter accurately, then you can be confident that the big idea is in your long-term memory, ready for the next time you need it.

Chapter 1

Psychology in Your Life

Welcome to the first chapter! In this section of the text, you'll learn about ideas that will set up many of the topics in the rest of the textbook, including what makes psychology a science, how these research findings can help you study and think critically, and how you can apply them to your personal and professional life. You'll also learn about the current state of psychological research and what methods researchers use to investigate thinking and behavior.

PRE-READING QUESTIONS

	ANSWER THESE QUESTIONS BEFORE you read the chapter. (You will refer to these answers again at the end of the chapter.)	REVISE YOUR ANSWERS NOW AFTER you read the chapter. Based on what you read in the chapter, revise your answer if needed.	Explain whether you predicted correctly or not, and what you know now that you didn't know before.
The way people learn and study best is specific to each individual, and there aren't useful general "rules" about how to study.	True False		
Modern psychological research can be divided into five domains: biological, cognitive, developmental, social/personality, and mental/physical health.	True False		
Psychological researchers can't really evaluate what causes thoughts or behaviors, because psychology is a subjective area of study.	True False		

RETRIEVE-AS-YOU-GO QUESTIONS

SECTION 1.1 Psychology Is a Science That Helps You Understand Your Mental Activity, Behavior, and Brain Processes

A. Define "psychology" in your own words.

B. Define "empiricism."

C. What makes psychology a science?

SECTION 1.2 Psychology Uses the Science of Learning to Help You Study Better

A. Define "growth mindset."

B. Define "self-regulated learning."

C. What are the elements of effective practice that improve learning?

D. How can the book's advice about attending and connecting help you think deeply?

SECTION 1.3 Psychology Develops Your Critical Thinking Skills

A. Define "critical thinking."

B. How does determining the source of a claim help you to think about it critically?

C. What counts as strong evidence for a claim?

D. Why is it important to search for multiple credible sources about a claim?

SECTION 1.4 Psychology Improves Your Life Personally and Professionally

A. What is one detail mentioned in the text that you can use to improve your life?

B. What is one detail mentioned in the text that you can use to get ahead in a job?

SECTION 1.5 Psychologists Investigate Topics Across Five Interconnected Domains

A. List the five domains of psychology.

B. Think of one topic or question that is an example of the intersection between the biological and mental and physical health domains.

C. Think of one topic or question that is an example of the intersection between the cognitive and developmental domains.

D. Think of one topic or question that is an example of the intersection between the social and personality and developmental domains.

SECTION 1.6 Psychology Is Becoming More Diverse

A. Provide one example of a way in which psychology is becoming a more diverse science.

B. Why is it important for researchers to include diverse participants in studies?

SECTION 1.7 Psychologists Must Be Ethical in Their Research

A. List the four ethical standards for psychological research.

B. Can any of the four ethical standards be altered for the sake of conducting very important research? Explain.

SECTION 1.8 Psychologists Use the Scientific Method

A. List the five steps of the scientific method.

B. Which steps in the scientific method involve figuring out how to gather data to test an explanation?

C. Which steps in the scientific method involve looking carefully at data and communicating conclusions?

SECTION 1.9 Descriptive Methods Describe What Is Happening

A. What is the overall purpose of all descriptive research methods?

B. Provide an example of a case study.

C. Provide an example of an observational study.

D. Provide an example of a self-report study.

SECTION 1.10 Correlational Methods Reveal Relationships

A. What is the overall purpose of all correlational research methods?	
B. List two variables that you suspect are correlated.	
C. Why can't we infer causation from correlational studies?	

SECTION 1.11 Experimental Methods Test Causation

A. What is the overall purpose of all experimental research methods?	
B. What is the relationship between independent and dependent variables in experiments?	
C. Why can experiments help researchers infer causation?	

Using Psychology in Your Life Consider an option that is personally relevant. (Page and chapter references are to *Psychology in Your Life*, Fourth High School Edition.)

1. Think of a person who has a growth mindset. How did their attitude help them manage disappointment and ultimately lead to success? (p. 6)

2. Test out attention research: Compare your productivity when studying with and without your phone in the room. Study for the same amount of time in each condition and compare your results (p. 8).

3. Describe a time you observed that an aspect of identity mentioned in section 1.6 affected academic expectations.

4. Check out the scientific method chart in Figure 1.17 (p. 26) and select one learning strategy (in Learning to Learn or Learning Pause) to use when studying for an assessment. After the assessment, evaluate the strategy's effectiveness.

5. Figure 1.24 shows examples in which news sources wrongly report correlations as causal claims. Scroll through your social media feeds and see if you can find an example of this. Record the claim and the source, and explain why the claim is false.

Key Takeaways What one new learning strategy will you use to maximize your learning for Chapter 1?

In Chapter 1, we learned about five primary domains of psychology: biological, mental and physical health, cognitive, developmental, social, and personality. Which do you find most compelling? Why?

THE BIG QUESTION

In general, what is the goal of the science of psychology? How do psychological researchers try to meet that goal?

Chapter 2
The Role of Biology in Psychology

Have you ever wondered how your brain works? In this chapter, you'll learn detailed information about how the neurons in your brain communicate, and how different parts of your brain all combine to make you, you! Along the way, you'll discover that beliefs many people hold about the brain are actually myths, and that the reality of brain structures and functions is more complex and mysterious than most people understand.

PRE-READING QUESTIONS

	ANSWER THESE QUESTIONS BEFORE you read the chapter. (You will refer to these answers again at the end of the chapter.)	REVISE YOUR ANSWERS NOW AFTER you read the chapter. Based on what you read in the chapter, revise your answer if needed.	Explain whether you predicted correctly or not, and what you know now that you didn't know before.
Biopsychologists can describe how our brain cells communicate.	True False		
The left hemisphere and right hemisphere of the brain control very different thinking/behavior functions.	True False		
The way in which our brain develops is controlled primarily by our genetics.	True False		

RETRIEVE-AS-YOU-GO QUESTIONS

SECTION 2.1 Your Nervous System Is the Basis of Your Mental Activity and Behavior

A. What is the difference between the central and peripheral nervous systems?

B. What is the relationship between neurons and the nervous system?

C. List the parts of a neuron.

SECTION 2.2 Neurons Communicate With Each Other in Your Nervous System

A. What happens during the transmission phase of neural transmission?

B. What happens during the reception phase of neural transmission?

C. What happens during the integration phase of neural transmission?

SECTION 2.3 Neurotransmitters Influence Your Mental Activity and Behavior

A. Explain what agonists do, and list two examples.

B. Explain what antagonists do, and list two examples.

C. What do serotonin and dopamine do? How are they similar? How are they different?

SECTION 2.4 Our Understanding of How the Brain Works Has Improved Over Time

A. How did the earliest brain researchers gather information about how the brain works?	
B. Explain what information an EEG provides about brain activity.	
C. Explain what information an fMRI provides about brain activity.	

SECTION 2.5 The Hindbrain and Midbrain House Basic Programs for Your Survival

A. How does the brain stem relate to how the brain functions?	
B. What does the medulla do?	
C. What does the cerebellum do?	

SECTION 2.6 Forebrain Subcortical Structures Control Your Motivations and Emotions

A. Contrast the functions of the thalamus and hypothalamus.	
B. What is the primary purpose of the hippocampus?	
C. What is the primary purpose of the amygdala?	

SECTION 2.7 The Cerebral Cortex of the Forebrain Processes Your Complex Mental Activity

A. How is the cerebral cortex different from all the other brain regions discussed in this chapter?

B. List the lobes of the cerebral cortex.

C. List three of the specialized cortexes of the brain and describe their primary function.

D. Why do biopsychologists think the prefrontal cortex is so important?

SECTION 2.8 The Hemispheres Work Together With Some Specialization

A. How do the left and right hemispheres communicate?

B. What is the impact of "split brain"?

C. What do researchers mean by the "left brain/right brain myth"?

SECTION 2.9 How Can You Succeed If You Have a Learning Disability?

A. Do most brains work in similar ways, or is every brain completely different?

B. Describe ADHD.

C. Describe dyslexia.

SECTION 2.10 The Peripheral Nervous System Includes the Somatic and Autonomic Systems

A. How is the somatic nervous system different from the autonomic nervous system?

B. Describe how the sympathetic and parasympathetic nervous systems react to emergencies.

C. Briefly explain three things your somatic nervous system is doing right now, and three things your autonomic nervous system is doing right now.

SECTION 2.11 The Endocrine System Affects Your Behavior Through Hormones

A. How are hormones different than neurotransmitters?

B. Describe one of the major endocrine glands in your body, and what hormone it secretes.

C. How do hormones affect the way in which you physically developed throughout your life?

SECTION 2.12 Your Genes Affect Your Mental Activity and Behavior

A. Briefly explain how genes and natural selection relate to evolutionary change.

B. What are some genes you know you inherited from your biological parents?

C. Why is "gene expression" important?

SECTION 2.13 Your Genes Interact With Your Environment to Influence You

A. Describe the purpose of behavioral genetics.	
B. Why are monozygotic and dizygotic twins important to behavioral geneticists?	
C. What does "epigenetics" mean?	

SECTION 2.14 Your Environment Changes Your Brain

A. Why is brain plasticity important?	
B. Do humans regrow neurons? How do we know?	
C. Can the brain reorganize itself? How do researchers know that it can or it can't?	

Using Psychology in Your Life Consider an option that is personally relevant. (Page and chapter references are to *Psychology in Your Life,* Fourth High School Edition.)

1. Figure 2.14 shows that your brain is organized into three main divisions: hindbrain, midbrain, and forebrain. Pick an after-school activity and explain how a part of each division is involved in successfully performing that activity.

2. Summarize the results of research about London cabbies described on page 65 (Maguire et al., 2003). Form a hypothesis about another before-and-after experiment you could do to test another area of the brain.

3. Figure 2.17 illustrates the four lobes of the cerebral cortex. Imagine that you could choose one to enhance in order to develop a superhuman power. Which would you choose? Why?

4. Chapter 2 contains numerous case studies viewed from the biological perspective. Select one case study to research further. Summarize your findings and cite your sources.

5. Behavioral geneticists use twin and adoption studies to learn about the interaction of nature and nurture. How do similarities and differences in your family shed light on this interaction?

Key Takeaways Considering recent research in brain plasticity and the Learning to Learn strategies on page 70, select one learning routine to use on a regular basis when studying the next chapter. Evaluate the impact on your recall and understanding.

The biological domain is involved in a wide variety of careers: "From Health Care to Marketing" describes just a few. Five years from now, what career path do you hope to be pursuing? What role does biological psychology play in this career?

THE BIG QUESTION

How do researchers uncover how the brain works, and what do you know about your brain now that you didn't know before?

Chapter 3
Consciousness

In Chapter 3, you will learn about both waking and altered states of consciousness, including those induced by sleep, drugs, and hypnosis. Thinking like a cognitive neuroscientist, you'll learn relevant findings about multitasking to be a more efficient student and meditation to help reduce stress. You'll also learn about trends in substance use and careers that address this societal issue.

PRE-READING QUESTIONS

	ANSWER THESE QUESTIONS BEFORE you read the chapter. (You will refer to these answers again at the end of the chapter.)	REVISE YOUR ANSWERS NOW AFTER you read the chapter. Based on what you read in the chapter, revise your answer if needed.	Explain whether you predicted correctly or not, and what you know now that you didn't know before.
Consciousness is nearly impossible to study because we can't use consciousness to study consciousness.	True False		
Sleeping is one of the most important and well-researched states of consciousness.	True False		
Altered states of consciousness result from psychoactive drugs and are inherently damaging.	True False		

RETRIEVE-AS-YOU-GO QUESTIONS

SECTION 3.1 Consciousness Is Your Subjective Experience

A. Define "consciousness."

B. Use the terms "objectivity" and "subjectivity" to explain why researchers stopped using the introspection method.

C. Contrast the two states of consciousness listed in the text.

SECTION 3.2 Consciousness Results From Brain Activity

A. What is the global workspace model?

B. How do traumatic brain injuries impact consciousness?

C. What does brain research indicate about comatose states?

SECTION 3.3 Consciousness Involves Attention

A. What are the elements of the "two-track mind" as described by Daniel Kahneman?

B. How does consciousness research relate to driving safety research?

C. Explain how inattentional blindness relates to research about multitasking.

SECTION 3.4 Unconscious Processing Sometimes Affects Behavior

A. What is subliminal perception?

B. According to research described in the text, how can subliminal messages impact our behavior?

SECTION 3.5 Consciousness Changes During Sleep

A. How does melatonin influence your circadian rhythm?

B. How does brain activity change during the four stages of sleep?

C. In what ways is REM different than the other sleep stages?

SECTION 3.6 People Dream While Sleeping

A. How are REM and non-REM dreams usually different?

B. What did Sigmund Freud believe dreams indicated?

C. What is the activation-synthesis theory of dreams?

SECTION 3.7 Sleep Is An Adaptive Behavior

A. Which three theories describe the benefits of sleep?

B. How does sleeping relate to effective studying?

C. Explain three impacts of sleep deprivation.

SECTION 3.8 How Can You Develop Better Sleep Habits?

A. List the eight recommendations in the text about sleep habits.

B. Which two recommendations are most relevant to your sleep habits?

SECTION 3.9 Sleep Disorders Are Relatively Common Throughout Life

A. What is insomnia, and how can people deal with it?

B. What is apnea, and how can people deal with it?

C. What is narcolepsy, and how can people deal with it?

D. What is REM behavior disorder, and how can people deal with it?

SECTION 3.10 Attention to Suggestions May Alter Consciousness in Hypnosis

A. Define "hypnosis" and "posthypnotic suggestion."

B. What kinds of people are most hypnotizable?

C. Explain the two theories of hypnosis.

SECTION 3.11 Meditation Alters Consciousness and Brain Functioning

A. What is mindfulness meditation?

B. What is concentration meditation?

C. According to brain research, how does meditation impact our brains?

SECTION 3.12 Psychoactive Drugs Affect the Brain

A. List the four categories of psychoactive drugs referenced in the chapter.

B. Explain the major physical impacts of each of the four categories of psychoactive drugs listed in the chapter.

C. Explain the risk of addiction of each of the four categories of psychoactive drugs listed in the chapter.

SECTION 3.13 Substance Use Disorder Has Physical and Psychological Aspects

A. Define "substance abuse disorder."	
B. Describe the relationship between tolerance and withdrawal.	
C. What are the risk factors for developing substance abuse disorder?	

Using Psychology in Your Life Consider an option that is personally relevant. (Page and chapter references are to *Psychology in Your Life*, Fourth High School Edition.)

1. Summarize Owen et al.'s study of a 23-year-old in a coma (p. 98). How might this impact a caregiver's ability to communicate with loved ones who are unresponsive?

2. For one week, check how many hours a day you spend on your phone. Describe and explain the correlation between your screen-time hours and your mood. How do your results compare with recent research about the negative effects of multitasking?

3. Laboratory research has confirmed that hypnosis can relieve pain. Would you seek hypnosis for pain relief during dental work or for a medical procedure? Why or why not?

4. Rank your stress level from one to ten. Find an online meditation practice to use at a similar time each day for 3 days. Rank your stress level afterward. How did your stress level change? Why?

5. Figure 3.33 shows the dramatic increase in fatal drug overdoses. Many high schools have Narcan available. Explain how Narcan works to help people survive an overdose.

Key Takeaways Chapter 3 highlights the importance of sleep on physical, cognitive, and mental health. Module 38 lists strategies to develop better sleep habits. Describe your current sleep habits and pick two strategies to try. Evaluate the results.

Cognitive neuroscientists who study consciousness draw from both biological and cognitive domains. Pick one altered state of consciousness and discuss the role that biological and cognitive (mental) factors play in an individual's experience of this state of consciousness.

THE BIG QUESTION

Overall, what do psychological researchers know about your current state of consciousness, and what influences it?

Chapter 4
Development Across the Life Span

In Chapter 4, you will learn about how people change and develop over the course of their lifetime. Developmental psychologists study the interaction between "nature" and "nurture" in order to explain physical, social, and cognitive development from the womb to the tomb. Research about biological factors like genes and heredity and environmental factors like parenting and social relationships shed light on how to live a full and healthy life no matter what your age.

PRE-READING QUESTIONS

	ANSWER THESE QUESTIONS BEFORE you read the chapter. (You will refer to these answers again at the end of the chapter.)	REVISE YOUR ANSWERS NOW AFTER you read the chapter. Based on what you read in the chapter, revise your answer if needed.	Explain whether you predicted correctly or not, and what you know now that you didn't know before.
Our motor development as a baby and child occurs mostly because of environmental influences, like parental encouragement and involvement in sports.	True False		
Some social, cognitive, and moral development occurs in predictable stages.	True False		
Cognitive problems such as confusion and memory loss are a normal, inevitable part of aging.	True False		

RETRIEVE-AS-YOU-GO QUESTIONS

SECTION 4.1 Humans Develop in Three Key Areas Starting in the Prenatal Period

A. List and describe the three developmental areas.

B. What important physical developmental changes occur during the germinal period?

C. What important physical developmental changes occur during the embryonic period?

D. What important physical developmental changes occur during the fetal period?

SECTION 4.2 There Are External Threats to Prenatal Development

A. Define "teratogens."

B. Which commonly used drugs are also teratogens?

C. What is microcephaly?

SECTION 4.3 Infants and Children Change Physically

A. Define "maturation."

B. What is neural pruning, why does it happen, and why is it important?

C. Describe how infants experience the world through their senses, and how that changes due to maturation.

SECTION 4.4 Infants and Children Change Socially and Emotionally

A. Define "attachment."

B. Contrast how Harlow and Ainsworth studied attachment.

C. List the attachment styles described by Ainsworth, and the possible impact of each style.

SECTION 4.5 Infants and Children Change Cognitively

A. Describe how schemas, assimilation, and accommodation contribute to cognitive development according to Piaget.

B. List the stages in Piaget's theory, along with at least one important cognitive development that occurs in each stage.

C. What is the theory of mind, and how does it relate to Piaget's theory?

SECTION 4.6 Language Develops in an Orderly Way

A. How do morphemes and phonemes relate to words?

B. List the stages of language development, along with one example of speech from each stage.

SECTION 4.7 Adolescents Develop Physically

A. How does our environment and hormonal changes contribute to puberty?	
B. What stage are adolescents working through, according to Piaget's theory? How does this stage relate to evidence from the text about decision-making?	
C. How might the changes in the limbic system relate to adolescent risk-taking and decision-making?	

SECTION 4.8 Adolescents Develop Socially and Emotionally

A. Explain the psychosocial challenge experienced by adolescents in Erikson's theory.	
B. Describe the different parenting styles in Baumrind's theory.	
C. Explain one of the criticisms of limitations of Baumrind's parenting styles theory.	

SECTION 4.9 What Roles Do Peers Play in Development?

A. Define "bullying" and list some of the types described in the text.	
B. What three steps does the text advise us to take if we experience or witness bullying?	

SECTION 4.10 Adolescents Develop Cognitively

A. Describe what the text calls "moral emotions."	
B. List the stages of Kohlberg's moral development theory.	
C. Explain one of the criticisms of Kohlberg's moral development theory.	

SECTION 4.11 Emerging Adulthood Is a New Developmental Period

A. Describe the emerging adulthood phase.	
B. Explain how societal changes over time contributed to the development of the emerging adulthood phase.	

SECTION 4.12 Bodies and Minds Change in Adulthood

A. How have life spans changed over time?	
B. Describe the cognitive impacts of aging.	

SECTION 4.13 Adults Develop Lifelong Social and Emotional Bonds

A. Explain the psychosocial challenge experienced by adults and older adults according to Erikson's theory.	
B. Drawing on research described in the text, summarize the physical and psychological impacts of long-term relationships for most people.	
C. Drawing on research described in the text, summarize the physical and psychological impacts of having children for most people.	

Using Psychology in Your Life Consider an option that is personally relevant. (Page and chapter references are to *Psychology in Your Life*, Fourth High School Edition.)

1. What kind of infant were you? Were you an "early" walker? A "late" talker? Ask a parent or guardian to describe your physical, cognitive, and social-emotional development from birth until you were 2 years old.

2. Test Piaget's four stages of cognitive development (Figure 4.15) on a child in your life. For example, you could ask a 3-year-old to play hide and seek to test egocentric thinking or ask a 6-year-old if two differently shaped glasses of water contained the same amount to test conservation. Record your findings.

3. In Erikson's eight stages of psychosocial development (Table 4.1), forming an identity in adolescence precedes forming a long-term relationship in adulthood. Do you agree? Is it necessary to establish your identity before finding a partner? Why or why not?

4. Should someone steal life-saving medication for their mother if they cannot afford to pay? Why or why not? How would Kohlberg and Haidt analyze your response?

5. Interview an older adult (65+) who plays a positive role in your life. Ask them what they do to maintain their physical, social, and cognitive health. Ask for their consent and record their responses.

Key Takeaways Developmental psychologists study the interaction of nature and nurture on development across the lifespan. Describe how you can promote physical, social, and cognitive health at your present stage. Give a specific example for each kind of development.

"Emerging adulthood" (covering ages 18–25) is a new developmental time period between adolescence and adulthood. Based on developmental research, what advice would you give to a recent college graduate hoping to live independently?

THE BIG QUESTION

What stages of development are you going through right now? Consider the three developmental areas and any developmental stage theories you consider relevant to your life.

Chapter 5
Sensation and Perception

In Chapter 5, you will learn how sensation and perception help us make sense of our world. You will learn about how humans see, hear, taste, smell, feel touch, and experience pain. While each sense is different in some ways, they follow a similar four-step process from detecting physical stimuli like light waves to organizing an idea like "I see an apple." Understanding how your senses work is useful as a student, athlete, performer, musician, and young adult.

PRE-READING QUESTIONS

	ANSWER THESE QUESTIONS BEFORE you read the chapter. (You will refer to these answers again at the end of the chapter.)	REVISE YOUR ANSWERS NOW AFTER you read the chapter. Based on what you read in the chapter, revise your answer if needed.	Explain whether you predicted correctly or not, and what you know now that you didn't know before.
Human experiences are so individually specific and complex that it is impossible to precisely describe how an individual senses the world.	True False		
All our senses are very similar: each sense absorbs energy, and that energy directly travels through the brain.	True False		
Our external anatomy (two eyes, two ears, etc.) includes important elements of our perception systems.	True False		

RETRIEVE-AS-YOU-GO QUESTIONS

SECTION 5.1 Your Senses Detect Physical Stimuli, and Your Brain Processes Perception

A. What is the difference between sensation and perception?	
B. What happens during the process of transduction?	
C. List three of the sensory cortexes and their location in the brain.	

SECTION 5.2 There Must Be a Certain Amount of a Stimulus for You to Detect It

A. Define "absolute threshold."	
B. Define "difference threshold."	
C. Explain how just-noticeable differences relate to Weber's law.	
D. Describe an example of sensory adaptation you've experienced.	

SECTION 5.3 Sensory Receptors in Your Eyes Detect Light

A. List the structures in the eye that allow you to see.	
B. What cells in the retina detect which kinds of light?	
C. How does the brain process sensory messages from the eye?	

SECTION 5.4 You Perceive Color Based on Physical Aspects of Light

A. Explain how trichromatic theory explains our perception of color.

B. Explain how opponent-process theory explains our perception of color.

SECTION 5.5 You Perceive Objects by Organizing Visual Information

A. What is the difference between bottom-up and top-down processing?

B. Explain an example of one of your perceptual sets.

C. How do the principles of figure—ground and grouping—relate to perceptual sets?

SECTION 5.6 When You Perceive Depth, You Can Locate Objects in Space

A. How does binocular disparity help with depth perception?

B. How do monocular cues help with depth perception?

C. Which kinds of depth cues do visual artists like painters use most often?

SECTION 5.7 Cues in Your Brain and in the World Let You Perceive Motion

A. What are motion aftereffects (aka the waterfall effect)?	
B. What is stroboscopic motion?	

SECTION 5.8 You Understand That Objects Remain Constant Even When Cues Change

A. Explain why object constancy is useful.	
B. How do size, shape, brightness, and color constancy relate to the overall idea of object constancy?	

SECTION 5.9 Receptors in Your Ears Detect Sound Waves

A. List the structures in the ear that allow you to hear.	
B. What cells in the ear detect what kind of energy?	
C. How does the brain process sensory messages from the ear?	

SECTION 5.10 How Can You Avoid Damage to Your Hearing from Listening to Loud Music With Earbuds?

A. What activities do you commonly experience that could damage your hearing if you were exposed to them for over 8 hours?	
B. What suggestions made in the text might be useful in your life?	

SECTION 5.11 You Perceive Sound Based on Physical Aspects of Sound Waves

A. How do amplitude and frequency relate to pitch and loudness?

B. Contrast how temporal and place coding both help describe how we perceive sound.

C. Use the term "localization" to explain why two ears are more useful than one.

D. How does the vestibular sense help us maintain our balance?

SECTION 5.12 Receptors in Your Taste Buds Detect Chemical Molecules

A. Explain the physical structures that enable us to taste.

B. What is one potential disadvantage of being a supertaster?

C. Are taste preferences determined mostly by nature or nurture?

SECTION 5.13 Your Olfactory Receptors Detect Odorants

A. Explain the physical structures that enable us to smell.

B. Explain this quote from the text: "olfaction has the most direct route to the brain."

C. What part of the olfaction process is still mysterious to researchers?

SECTION 5.14 Receptors in Your Skin Detect Temperature and Pressure

A. List the different kinds of touch receptors in our skin.	
B. What brain region is responsible for touch sensations?	
C. Contrast the kinesthetic sense with the sense of touch.	

SECTION 5.15 You Detect Pain in Your Skin and Throughout Your Body

A. Which two nerve fibers are responsible for which types of pain perceptions?	
B. How does gate control theory explain how we experience pain?	

Using Psychology in Your Life Consider an option that is personally relevant. (Page and chapter references are to *Psychology in Your Life*, Fourth High School Edition.)

1. Some motorcyclists have a bumper sticker that says, "Look Twice, Save a Life." Explain how this bumper sticker relates to Figure 5.6, "Find Your Blind Spot."

2. Figures 5.14 and 5.15 show two examples of perceptual sets. Describe an example from your own life that illustrates how perceptual sets are a form of top-down processing.

3. Sketch a social scene similar to Figure 5.17 and identify three monocular cues that you used to create depth.

4. What's your favorite music genre? Figure 5.22 illustrates how you hear in four steps. Explain how you hear a song in this genre following these four steps.

5. Test gender differences in smell. Blindfold six participants (three male and three female) and ask them to identify five everyday items. Record your results. Do they support research that females are generally better than males at identifying odors?

Key Takeaways The Hearing Education and Awareness for Rockers (HEAR) organization estimates that 60 percent of Rock & Roll Hall of Fame inductees are hard of hearing. Check your smartphone for your weekly audio exposure and assess impact on your hearing. Select a strategy from Using Psychology in Your Life 5.10 (p. 200) to prevent damage.

The four-step process (Figure 5.1), starting with receptor cells detecting physical stimuli and ending with the brain interpreting meaning, highlights an important theme in psychology: nature interacts with nurture. Pick one sense from Chapter 5 and give a specific example from your life how you developed this sense via nature and nurture.

THE BIG QUESTION

Plato said that humans are separated from the world by a "wall of senses." Use what you learned about sensation and perception in this chapter to explain what you think Plato meant by this statement.

Chapter 6
Learning

Psychologists use the term "learning" in a different way than we've heard it used in school. The behavioral-psychological perspective focuses on how we are conditioned to behave through associating different stimuli or through rewards (reinforcements) or punishments. However, more recent research highlights how our thinking, biology, and ability to observe others enhance our ability to learn new behaviors.

PRE-READING QUESTIONS

	ANSWER THESE QUESTIONS BEFORE you read the chapter. (You will refer to these answers again at the end of the chapter.)	REVISE YOUR ANSWERS NOW AFTER you read the chapter. Based on what you read in the chapter, revise your answer if needed.	Explain whether you predicted correctly or not, and what you know now that you didn't know before.
Classical conditioning involves an organism associating two stimuli with an automatic response.	True False		
Operant conditioning is the more accurate and updated theory of conditioning.	True False		
Observational learning is one of the abilities that defines the difference between humans and non-human animals.	True False		

RETRIEVE-AS-YOU-GO QUESTIONS

SECTION 6.1 You Learn from Experience

A. Define "learning."

B. What was John Watson's claim about how humans learn?

C. In what way do modern psychologists disagree with Watson about learning?

SECTION 6.2 You Learn in Three Ways

A. What are the three types of learning?

B. Contrast habituation and sensitization.

C. Provide an example of associative learning.

D. Provide an example of observational learning.

SECTION 6.3 Through Classical Conditioning, You Learn That Stimuli Are Related

A. Define "classical conditioning."

B. What is the relationship between an unconditioned stimulus and an unconditioned response?

C. What is the relationship between a conditioned stimulus and a conditioned response?

D. Explain the role of a neutral stimulus in the classical conditioning process.

SECTION 6.4 Learning Varies in Classical Conditioning

A. What happens during the acquisition phase of classical conditioning?

B. What causes a classically conditioned response to become extinct?

C. Describe an example of spontaneous recovery.

D. Contrast stimulus generalization and stimulus discrimination.

SECTION 6.5 You Can Learn Fear Responses Through Classical Conditioning

A. Explain how Little Albert was conditioned.

B. What is the goal of counterconditioning?

SECTION 6.6 Adaptation and Cognition Influence Classical Conditioning

A. How do conditioned taste aversions challenge Ivan Pavlov's original theory of classical conditioning?

B. According to Robert Rescorla, how is cognition involved in classical conditioning?

SECTION 6.7 Through Operant Conditioning, You Learn the Consequences of Your Actions

A. Define "operant conditioning."

B. Define "reinforcer."

C. What is the purpose of a Skinner box?

SECTION 6.8 You Can Improve Learning Through Reinforcement

A. What is the purpose of shaping?

B. Contrast primary and secondary reinforcers.

C. Describe how generalization and discrimination work in the context of operant conditioning?

SECTION 6.9 Both Reinforcement and Punishment Can Influence Behavior

A. How is positive reinforcement similar to positive punishment?

B. How is negative reinforcement similar to negative punishment?

C. Why would a psychologist use a schedule of reinforcement?

SECTION 6.10 Positive Punishment Is Often Ineffective

A. Provide an example of positive punishment.

B. Why is positive reinforcement more likely to be effective at improving behavior than positive punishment?

C. Summarize the research about the impacts of spanking.

SECTION 6.11 Can Behavior Modification Help You Learn to Exercise Regularly?

A. Define "behavior modification."

B. How are secondary reinforcements used to establish a token economy?

C. What is the role of positive reinforcement in the six-step reinforcement recommendation listed in the text?

SECTION 6.12 Biology and Cognition Influence Operant Conditioning

A. What is the role of dopamine in operant conditioning?

B. What is the role of evolutionary adaptation in operant conditioning?

C. How did Edward Tolman's research indicate that cognition plays a role in operant conditioning?

A. Define "observational learning."	
B. What was the goal of Albert Bandura's Bobo doll study?	
C. What factors influence whether we will model the behaviors of others?	
D. How does vicarious learning relate to observational learning?	

SECTION 6.14 Biology Influences Observational Learning

A. What are mirror neurons?	
B. How might mirror neurons influence observational learning?	

Using Psychology in Your Life Consider an option that is personally relevant. (Page and chapter references are to *Psychology in Your Life*, Fourth High School Edition.)

1. Pavlov's experiments revealed four steps of classical conditioning (p. 226). Use the four steps to explain a time when you developed a taste aversion by eating something that made you sick.

2. Describe something that terrifies you. How could you use Mary Cover Jones's method of counterconditioning to reduce your fear?

3. Figure 6.16 shows a dog surfing. Describe another cool pet trick. Explain how to use shaping to train an animal to perform this trick.

4. Pick a public person you follow on social media. Chart the responses to their posts for 24 hours. What patterns do you notice? What types of behaviors elicit favorable responses? Unfavorable ones?

5. Figure 6.26 shows Bandura's classic observational learning research. Watch a children's program and record the main character's behaviors as aggressive, prosocial, or neutral. Evaluate the possible impact of the show on the child's behavior.

Key Takeaways Operant conditioning can help you achieve your personal, academic, and social goals. Identify a specific and measurable goal. Use the six-step behavior modification program on page 245 for a period of three weeks to achieve your goal.

Write a thank you note to someone who is a positive role model in your life. In your note describe research about observational learning and explain what you've learned from them.

THE BIG QUESTION

What do you think influences your behavior most? Classical conditioning? Operant conditioning? Observational learning? Explain your answer.

Chapter 7
Memory

Since you are a student, psychological research about how your memory system works may be the most valuable research in this textbook! This chapter summarizes some of the main theories about the structure and process of your memory system. You will also learn about what researchers know so far about how memories are stored in the brain, and what happens when those brain processes are disrupted.

PRE-READING QUESTIONS

	ANSWER THESE QUESTIONS BEFORE you read the chapter. (You will refer to these answers again at the end of the chapter.)	REVISE YOUR ANSWERS NOW AFTER you read the chapter. Based on what you read in the chapter, revise your answer if needed.	Explain whether you predicted correctly or not, and what you know now that you didn't know before.
Human memory systems are highly individualized, and each person needs to discover the best memory techniques that fit their learning style.	*True False*		
The dominant theory of memory involves a process of three overall memory "stores."	*True False*		
Researchers haven't yet discovered much about how a memory is physically stored in brain neurons once it is encoded.	*True False*		

RETRIEVE-AS-YOU-GO QUESTIONS

SECTION 7.1 You Create Memories by Processing Information

A. Define "memory."

B. Define "encoding."

C. Describe the storage and retrieval phases on memory.

SECTION 7.2 Your Memories Are Unique

A. Describe one of the ways human memory is different than computer memory.

B. Define "selective attention."

C. How does the cocktail party effect relate to the filter effect and selective attention?

SECTION 7.3 You Maintain Information in Three Memory Stores

A. Describe the three memory stores.

B. What is the purpose of sensory memory?

C. What is the purpose of short-term memory?

D. What is the purpose of long-term memory?

SECTION 7.4 Sensory Storage Lets You Maintain Information Very Briefly

A. How did George Sperling's research establish the nature of sensory memory?

B. Explain how sensory memory helps us experience the world.

SECTION 7.5 Working Memory Lets You Actively Maintain Information in Short-Term Storage

A. Compare short-term memory to working memory.

B. Describe the duration and capacity of short-term memory.

C. How does chunking relate to working memory and the capacity of short-term memory?

SECTION 7.6 Long-Term Storage Lets You Maintain Memories Relatively Permanently

A. Contrast maintenance and elaborative rehearsal.

B. Explain which kind of encoding is more effective for long-term storage: visual, acoustic, or semantic.

C. Use the terms "primacy effect" and "recency effect" to define the serial position effect.

SECTION 7.7 Your Long-Term Storage Is Organized Based on Meaning

A. How do schemas influence our long-term memory and retrieval?

B. What are association networks?

SECTION 7.8 There Are Two Types of Amnesia

A. Which brain structures are usually involved in cases of amnesia?

B. What is the difference between anterograde and retrograde amnesia?

SECTION 7.9 Your Explicit Memories Involve Conscious Effort

A. What is the primary difference between explicit and implicit memory?

B. What are the two types of explicit memories?

C. What are the two types of implicit memories?

SECTION 7.10 Your Implicit Memories Function Without Conscious Effort

A. Why were patient H.M.'s explicit memories affected by his amnesia, but his implicit memories weren't?

B. In what ways are procedural memories "unconscious"?

SECTION 7.11 Memory Is Processed by Several Regions of Your Brain

A. List the brain structures involved in our memory system.

B. What is long-term potentiation?

C. What roles do consolidation and reconsolidation play in our memory system?

SECTION 7.12 Retrieval Cues Help You Access Your Memories

A. How does state-dependent memory relate to context-dependent memory?

B. What is prospective memory?

C. Why do mnemonic devices help us retrieve memories?

SECTION 7.13 You Forget Some of Your Memories

A. Why is forgetting an important part of the memory system?

B. What is the difference between retroactive and proactive interference?

C. Provide an example of blocking.

SECTION 7.14 Your Memories Can Be Distorted

A. What influences memory bias?

B. Are flashbulb memories accurate? How does research test this question?

C. What is source amnesia?

D. Explain what Loftus's research indicates about eyewitness testimony.

Using Psychology in Your Life Consider an option that is personally relevant. (Page and chapter references are to *Psychology in Your Life*, Fourth High School Edition.)

1. Figure 7.2 shows that limited attention impairs memory. Ask three friends how they ignore irrelevant distractions (like social media) in class and while completing homework. Compare their techniques and select the one that seems the most effective to try for a week.

2. How many phone contacts do you have? How many phone numbers can you remember? Pick three important numbers (such as those of a parent or guardian, or an emergency contact) and use elaborative rehearsal (p. 270) to commit these numbers to memory. Describe your strategy.

3. Figure 7.13, "A Network of Associations," shows how concepts are organized in long-term memory. Draw a network to illustrate how Figure 7.22, "Brain Regions Associated With Memory," is connected to Chapter 2, "The Role of Biology in Psychology." Include at least three parts of the brain in your diagram.

4. The main character in *Memento*, a mystery thriller film, suffers from amnesia. Watch the film or trailer and compare his experience with H.M.'s case of anterograde amnesia. How realistic is the movie's portrayal of memory loss?

5. Describe one of your first episodic memories. How old were you? If you can, ask a family member to also recall the event. Explain why your memory is most likely not entirely accurate.

Key Takeaways Chapter 7 contains many relevant strategies to improve your memory, including monitoring (p. 263), elaborating (p. 270), mnemonics (p. 288), and connecting (p. 289). Create a study plan that uses three terms from this unit to study for the unit test. After the test, evaluate your results and select one memory strategy to use for upcoming tests.

Imagine a good friend is interested in a career in criminal justice because they want to protect innocent people. They believe that eyewitness testimony is the most effective way to solve crimes and prevent harm. Correct this misconception by explaining why eyewitness accounts are often inaccurate. Use Elizabeth Loftus's research and the terms "misattribution" and "suggestibility" to support your argument.

THE BIG QUESTION

Out of all the memory concepts and theories you learned in this chapter, which one do you think is the most important for your success as a student? Why?	

Chapter 8
Thinking and Intelligence

Since psychology is the science of thinking and behavior, it's not surprising that there is a large body of psychology research dedicated to the study of thinking itself. In this chapter, you will learn about the basic components of your thought processes as well as problem solving techniques (in addition to some obstacles that get in your way during problem solving). Measuring intelligence is a challenge for researchers, involving controversies, specific requirements, and criteria.

PRE-READING QUESTIONS

	ANSWER THESE QUESTIONS BEFORE you read the chapter. (You will refer to these answers again at the end of the chapter.)	REVISE YOUR ANSWERS NOW AFTER you read the chapter. Based on what you read in the chapter, revise your answer if needed.	Explain whether you predicted correctly or not, and what you know now that you didn't know before.
Concepts, schemas, and stereotypes are all related and form the basis of human thinking processes.	True False		
Researchers agree that intelligence should be measured as a single construct, instead of multiple categories.	True False		
Intelligence is studied by cognitive psychologists rather than biological or neurological researchers.	True False		

RETRIEVE-AS-YOU-GO QUESTIONS

SECTION 8.1 Thinking Is the Mental Manipulation of Representations

A. How does thinking relate to mental representations?

B. Explain the difference between analogical and symbolic representations.

C. Provide an example from your life when you used a mental map.

SECTION 8.2 Schemas and Concepts Are the Basis of Thinking

A. Explain the relationship between schemas and concepts.

B. List your prototype for the mental concept "psychological researcher."

C. How is the exemplar model different than the prototype model?

SECTION 8.3 Schemas Are the Basis of Stereotypes

A. What is the relationship between a schema and a stereotype?

B. Explain an example of a useful stereotype.

C. How could you avoid using an inaccurate stereotype in your thinking about others?

SECTION 8.4 Biased Reasoning Can Lead to Faulty Beliefs

A. Contrast formal and informal reasoning.

B. Define "confirmation bias."

C. How is an illusory correlation different from actual examples of correlation?

D. Provide an example of a time when you think you used hindsight bias.

SECTION 8.5 How You Think Biases Decision Making

A. Why do people use heuristics during decision making?

B. Provide an example of the availability heuristic.

C. Provide an example of the representativeness heuristic.

D. Explain the influence of the framing effect.

SECTION 8.6 How Can You Be Satisfied with Big Decisions?

A. Describe the difference between "maximizing" and "satisficing," and how they relate to feelings of satisfaction with decisions.

B. Explain how you might use the four pieces of advice about achieving satisfaction with decisions in your life.

SECTION 8.7 You Solve Problems to Achieve Goals

A. How can using subgoals help when solving problems?

B. How can working backwards help to solve a problem?

C. How can analogies help during problem solving?

D. Explain the role of insight in problem solving.

SECTION 8.8 You Overcome Obstacles to Solve Problems

A. How is restructuring used to solve problems?

B. Explain an example of a mental set interfering with problem solving.

C. Define "functional fixedness."

SECTION 8.9 One General Factor May Underlie Intelligence

A. Define "intelligence."

B. Summarize the current research findings about general intelligence.

C. How is fluid intelligence different from crystallized intelligence?

SECTION 8.10 There May Be Alternative Types of Intelligence

A. Explain the difference between convergent and divergent thinking.

B. Summarize Howard Gardner's multiple intelligence theory.

C. Summarize Robert Sternberg's triarchic intelligence theory.

D. What positive outcomes are correlated with high emotional intelligence?

SECTION 8.11 Intelligence Is a Result of Genes and Environment

A. Define "behavioral genetics."

B. Explain how researchers use twin studies to investigate intelligence.

C. List some environmental factors that may influence intelligence.

SECTION 8.12 Intelligence Is Assessed with Psychometric Tests

A. Explain how reliability and validity relate to intelligence tests.

B. Contrast aptitude and achievement tests.

C. How do IQ tests relate to the normal distribution?	
D. How do intelligence tests try to avoid cultural bias?	

SECTION 8.13 Intelligence Is Associated with Cognitive Performance

A. Explain the relationship between reaction time and intelligence.	
B. Explain the relationship between working memory and intelligence.	
C. What does research about savants indicate about the nature of intelligence?	

Using Psychology in Your Life Consider an option that is personally relevant. (Page and chapter references are to *Psychology in Your Life,* Fourth High School Edition.)

1. Explain the significance of the "before" and "after" depictions in "A Teen Draws a Scientist" (Figure 8.8). How do stereotypes relate to problems with eyewitness testimony described in Chapter 7?

2. Figure 8.11 charts the relationship between global temperature and piracy. Why is this an illusory correlation? Give an example of an illusory correlation in the news or in your life, such as superstitious behaviors before big games.

3. Psychologists use divergent thinking tests to assess creativity. Test three friends by asking each to list as many uses for a fork as they can in one minute. Record and evaluate your results. Is this a valid measure of creativity? Why or why not?

4. Table 8.3, "Dimensions of Intelligence," describes key characteristics of six theories of intelligence. Which theory best characterizes intelligence? Which theory is least biased? Defend your view with evidence from Chapter 8.

5. A friend says, "I'm not smart enough to go to college. No one in my family went. I'm sure I'd fail an IQ test." Explain why their thinking is inaccurate using terms from Section 8.12.

Key Takeaways Evaluating bias: Pick a current event and watch the way in which two news sources with differing perspectives cover it. Take notes, recording as objectively as possible names of speakers, specific claims, and supporting evidence. Analyze your notes to find examples of biased reasoning (confirmation bias, illusory correlations, hindsight bias) and decision making (availability and/or representative heuristic and framing). Discuss your conclusions.

Iyengar and Lepper's research (Figure 8.14) shows that too much choice can inhibit decision making. Identify a major decision in your life where you have a variety of choices. Use psychologist Barry Schwartz's four-step process (p. 317) to help make this decision. Recent research especially supports Schwartz's fourth step, "practice an attitude of gratitude." You can test this research by writing three things that you're grateful for each day for a week.

THE BIG QUESTION

One of the key aspects of the definition of intelligence is problem solving. How do problem-solving techniques and obstacles relate to the way in which you solve problems?

Chapter 9
Motivation and Emotion

When people use the phrase "human nature," they are usually making a claim about what motivates people to act in a certain way. In this chapter, you'll learn about several competing theories about what motivates human behaviors. Human motivation is complex, and these theories acknowledge that complexity by attempting to explain different categories of behaviors. The end of the chapter focuses on theories about emotions, including the relationship between how we feel and physiological changes.

PRE-READING QUESTIONS

	ANSWER THESE QUESTIONS BEFORE you read the chapter. (You will refer to these answers again at the end of the chapter.)	REVISE YOUR ANSWERS NOW AFTER you read the chapter. Based on what you read in the chapter, revise your answer if needed.	Explain whether you predicted correctly or not, and what you know now that you didn't know before.
Humans are primarily motivated by biological drives, like hunger, rather than cognitive drives, like achievement.	True False		
The right level of arousal can enhance performance.	True False		
Emotions impact physiological reactions, and physiological reactions can impact emotions.	True False		

RETRIEVE-AS-YOU-GO QUESTIONS

SECTION 9.1 Many Factors Influence Motivation

A. Define "motivation" in your own words.	
B. What is the main idea of Maslow's hierarchy of needs?	
C. How would drive reduction theory explain your current state of hunger?	
D. Explain how the optimum level of arousal relates to the Yerkes-Dodson law.	

SECTION 9.2 Some Behaviors Are Motivated for Their Own Sake

A. Contrast intrinsic and extrinsic motivation.	
B. Explain how extrinsic rewards can reduce intrinsic motivation.	
C. Define "self-determination theory" in your own words.	

SECTION 9.3 Motivation to Eat Is Affected by Biology

A. List the biological mechanisms involved in hunger.	
B. What parts of the brain control what aspects of hunger?	

SECTION 9.4 Motivation to Eat Is Also Influenced by Learning

A. How can classical conditioning impact hunger?

B. Explain how food familiarity and cultural influences impact what we eat.

C. How did human evolution influence food preferences?

SECTION 9.5 People Have a Need to Belong

A. Explain how the need to belong might influence behaviors at your school.

B. How can "belonging uncertainty" relate to mental health?

SECTION 9.6 People Have a Need to Achieve Long-Term Goals

A. Explain achievement motivation theory in your own words.

B. How is self-efficacy different from self-esteem?

C. What did Walter Mischel's marshmallow test research indicate about the benefits of the ability to delay gratification?

SECTION 9.7 Emotions Are Personal but Labeled and Described Consistently

A. Define "emotion" in your own words.

B. Contrast primary and secondary emotions.

C. Explain how the circumplex model categorizes emotions.

SECTION 9.8 Three Major Theories Explain Your Emotions

A. What is the major difference between the James-Lange and the Canon-Bard theories of emotions?

B. Explain the two-factor theory of emotions using an example from your life.

SECTION 9.9 Your Body and Brain Influence Your Emotions

A. What does cross-cultural research reveal about the relationship between bodily responses and emotions?

B. How effective is a polygraph at detecting lies?

C. Briefly describe how emotions are processed in the brain via the "fast path" and the "second path."

SECTION 9.10 Most People Try to Regulate Their Emotional States

A. Which of these emotion-regulation techniques do you use more often: thought suppression or positive reappraisal?	
B. Which of these emotion-regulation techniques do you use more often: humor or distraction?	

SECTION 9.11 You Use Facial Expressions to Interpret Emotions

A. How did Ekman investigate whether facial expressions are similar across cultures? What did that research reveal?	
B. Define "display rules" in your own words.	

SECTION 9.12 Emotions Strengthen Your Interpersonal Relations

A. Explain how guilt can strengthen social bonds.	
B. How do emotion researchers explain blushing?	

Using Psychology in Your Life Consider an option that is personally relevant. (Page and chapter references are to *Psychology in Your Life*, Fourth High School Edition.)

1. Describe three reasons why you want to earn a good grade in psychology class. Classify each reason as extrinsically or intrinsically motivated. Considering the research that extrinsic rewards can reduce motivation (p. 350), pick the reason that will lead to the most effective efforts.

2. A friend is moving and worried about feeling isolated at their new school. What research could you share about ways to increase belonging (p. 358) that could help ease their fear? Format your answer as an email or text reply.

3. Will Smith's comment "I will not be outworked, period," (Figure 9.16) illustrates the persistence that leads to achievement. Interview a person in your life who has grit. Record your interview and highlight a motivational quote from the interview to share.

4. A friend wants to finally ask their crush out. Describe the two-factor theory and apply Dutton and Aron's findings (Figure 9.23) on misattribution of arousal to plan an epic first date.

5. Describe a situation that made you extremely angry. In your description, include details about your immediate and long-term responses. Section 9.10 describes research-based techniques to manage emotions. Explain how you could use positive reappraisal, humor, or distraction to alleviate your anger.

Key Takeaways What's one major goal you want to accomplish this year? Dream big and imagine that whatever you write down will come true. Research shows that four factors improve your ability to achieve goals: the goals themselves, your self-efficacy, your ability to delay gratification, and your grit. Select two factors and create a road map to achieve your goal.

"From Sales to Financial Services" (p. 373) highlights how understanding motivation and emotion is useful in many careers. Describe how what you've learned about motivation and emotion is helpful in a leadership role that you play, whether it be at your job, on a sports team, during your extracurriculars, or in the classroom.

THE BIG QUESTION

Of all the motivating factors you read about in this chapter, which ones do you think motivate you most in your life choices? Is there a theory that you believe explains most of your motivations best?

Chapter 10
Sex, Gender, and Sexuality

Gender and sexual identity may seem clear and straightforward, but when psychological researchers ask large samples of people about how they think about their gender identities and experience sexual desire, they discover a wide variety of responses. In this chapter you will learn about ways to think about how humans describe their gender and sexual orientation, as well as research regarding how to support others who experience gender and sexual attraction differently than you do.

PRE-READING QUESTIONS

	ANSWER THESE QUESTIONS BEFORE you read the chapter. (You will refer to these answers again at the end of the chapter.)	REVISE YOUR ANSWERS NOW AFTER you read the chapter. Based on what you read in the chapter, revise your answer if needed.	Explain whether you predicted correctly or not, and what you know now that you didn't know before.
Biologically, there are two sexes, but psychologically, there are many genders.	True False		
Social, cognitive, genetic, and hormonal factors influence our gender identities.	True False		
The most useful way to think about gender is as a continuum, rather than discrete categories.	True False		

RETRIEVE-AS-YOU-GO QUESTIONS

SECTION 10.1 Genetics and Hormones Are Aspects of Biological Sex

A. List some of the genetic aspects of biological sex.	
B. List some of the hormonal aspects of biological sex.	
C. Briefly explain how chromosomes lead to the genetic and hormonal aspects of sex.	

SECTION 10.2 Some People Experience Variations in Biological Aspects of Sex

A. How common are differences in sexual development (DSDs)?	
B. How do chromosomes relate to DSDs?	
C. How do hormones relate to DSDs?	

SECTION 10.3 Thoughts About Gender Affect Our Perceptions, Expectations, and Actions

A. Define "gender schema" in your own words.	
B. How can gender schema lead to gender stereotypes?	
C. Explain an example of gender role socialization you experienced in your life.	

SECTION 10.4 Gender Identity Is How You Think and Feel About Your Own Gender

A. Define "gender identity" in your own words.

B. How does cognitive development theory explain how we form gender identities?

SECTION 10.5 People Vary in Gender Identity

A. Explain the terms "cisgender" and "transgender" in your own words.

B. What is the difference between gender dysmorphia, being transgender, and having a non-binary gender identity?

C. What legal protections are in place to protect the rights of transgender or gender-nonconforming people?

SECTION 10.6 How Can You Support People of All Gender Identities?

A. List three of the recommendations from the text regarding how you can support people of all gender identities.

B. Explain how you might use one of the recommendations in your life.

SECTION 10.7 Variations in Sexual Orientation Are Common

A. Define "sexual orientation" in your own words.

B. Explain what it means to think about sexual orientation as a continuum.

SECTION 10.8 Sexual Orientation Has a Biological Basis

A. How can our social environment influence a person's public expression of sexual orientation?

B. Explain some evidence for genetic influence on sexual orientation.

C. Explain some evidence for hormonal influence on sexual orientation.

D. How has the psychiatric community changed its view of "homosexuality" over time?

SECTION 10.9 Biology Influences the Motivation for Sexual Activity

A. Describe the steps in the sexual response cycle.

B. How do hormones contribute to sexual desire and behavior?

SECTION 10.10 Environmental Context Influences the Motivation for Sexual Activity

A. How have rates of sex outside of marriage changed over time?

B. What are some negative outcomes associated with viewing pornography?

C. Define "affirmative consent" in your own words.

A. Define "paraphilic disorder" in your own words.	
B. What are the most common sexual dysfunctions reported by people who identify as women, and for people who identify as men?	

Using Psychology in Your Life Consider an option that is personally relevant. (Page and chapter references are to *Psychology in Your Life*, Fourth High School Edition.)

1. Imagine that you're a camp counselor for a group of 10-year-olds. A girl feels embarrassed to put on her swimsuit because she is developing breasts earlier than others. How would you explain puberty to her in a comforting and scientific way?

2. A grandparent recently saw a program about transgender people in the military and tells you that they find the topic difficult to accept. Describe recent scientific research about the biological aspects of sex beyond the binary categories of male and female to help your grandparent develop understanding.

3. Figure 10.7 highlights the way that kids' toys are becoming more flexible around gender. Describe, in detail, one of your favorite toys from childhood. How did you play with it? Did your toy reinforce gender stereotypes or was it more gender fluid?

4. A classmate believes that sexual orientation is a choice, claiming another classmate "came out to get attention." Correct this misconception by describing the biological basis of sexual orientation.

5. As part of a mentoring program, you are asked to talk to middle schoolers about affirmative consent and healthy sexual relationships. Your talk should include research in a way that early teens can understand. What would you say?

Key Takeaways Scientific research about sex, gender, and sexual orientation provides ample evidence to challenge our preexisting beliefs and better understand the rich variety of human experiences. Reflect on your Chapter 10 learning. What surprised you? What section did you find most meaningful? What are you still curious about?

Young people in the LGBTQ community are more at risk for mental health concerns including suicidality. Thankfully, there are ways to support teens: "Human Services and Social Work" (p. 410) highlights supportive careers. Section 10.6 lists APA guidelines to support people of all gender identities and describes The Trevor Project, a crisis intervention and suicide prevention organization (pp. 402–403). Research one of these supports in more detail. Summarize your findings.

THE BIG QUESTION

You learned about several different ways to categorize gender identity and sexual orientation in this chapter. Which of these categorization methods best match your life experience? Why?

Chapter 11
Health and Well-Being

When you think about questions related to your health and wellness, you might be more likely to consider consulting a medical doctor than a psychological researcher. But psychological research establishes many useful lessons about our physical, emotional, and cognitive health. In this chapter you'll learn about the impacts of stress, the causes and effects of specific health-related behaviors, and what the "positive psychologists" may have to teach us about increasing our overall well-being.

PRE-READING QUESTIONS

	ANSWER THESE QUESTIONS BEFORE you read the chapter. (You will refer to these answers again at the end of the chapter.)	REVISE YOUR ANSWERS NOW AFTER you read the chapter. Based on what you read in the chapter, revise your answer if needed.	Explain whether you predicted correctly or not, and what you know now that you didn't know before.
Since psychology is the science of thinking and behavior, researchers focus on mental illness rather than more general "health" questions.	True False		
Motivations for some specific unhealthy behaviors (and the most successful methods of quitting) are established by research.	True False		
All stress by definition is harmful to our overall health.	True False		

RETRIEVE-AS-YOU-GO QUESTIONS

SECTION 11.1 Biology, Psychology, and Social Factors Influence Your Health

A. What kinds of research questions are health psychologists interested in?

B. Explain how the biopsychosocial model relates to well-being.

C. How do racial and ethnic biases impact well-being?

SECTION 11.2 Obesity Has Many Health Consequences

A. Define "obesity" in your own words.

B. Describe an example of a psychological factor that impacts overeating.

C. What is the evidence for social transmission of obesity?

D. Describe the cycle of restrictive dieting.

SECTION 11.3 Exercise Benefits You Physically, Cognitively, and Emotionally

A. Explain one of the benefits of exercise for physical health.

B. Explain one of the benefits of exercise for cognition.

C. Explain one of the benefits of exercise for emotions/mood.

SECTION 11.4 Sexually Transmitted Infections Can Be Prevented by Practicing Safer Sex

A. List three of the most common STIs and their treatments.

B. Explain one of the aspects of safer sex and how it can help prevent STIs.

C. What are the barrier methods of protection against STIs?

SECTION 11.5 Smoking Is Dangerous to Your Health

A. What motivates people to continue smoking?

B. Is vaping more or less harmful than smoking traditional cigarettes?

C. What is the most commonly successful method of quitting smoking?

SECTION 11.6 There Is Stress in Daily Life

A. How does eustress differ from distress?

B. Contrast the health impacts of daily hassles and major life stressors.

SECTION 11.7 You Can Have Several Responses to Stress

A. Describe the stages of the general adaptation syndrome (GAS).

B. How do short-term and long-term stress impact the immune system?

C. Contrast the fight-or-flight and the tend-and-befriend responses.

SECTION 11.8 Personality and Emotional States Influence the Impact of Stress on Heart Disease

A. What are the differences between type A and type B behavior patterns?

B. What components of the type A behavior pattern are linked with heart disease?

SECTION 11.9 Coping Mediates the Impact of Stress

A. Describe Lazarus's two-part appraisal process.

B. Which is more effective: emotion-focused or problem-focused coping? Why?

C. Explain one way that resilience helps people cope with stress.

SECTION 11.10 How Can You Reduce Exam Anxiety?

A. How does the stress of an upcoming test relate to the three components of stress?

B. Which of the four test anxiety coping strategies listed in the text might be most useful to you? Why?

SECTION 11.11 Positive Psychology Emphasizes Well-Being

A. What are the goals of positive psychology?

B. How does well-being relate to personal motivation?

C. Define "mindfulness" in your own words.

SECTION 11.12 Social Support Is Associated With Good Health

A. How does social support relate to physical health?

B. What health outcomes are associated with gratitude?

C. How might religion help people cope with distress?

SECTION 11.13 Several Strategies Can Help You Stay Healthy

A. According to advice in the text, what are some physical changes you could make to improve your health?

B. According to advice in the text, what are some psychological or emotional changes you could make to improve your health?

Using Psychology in Your Life: Consider an option that is personally relevant. (Page and chapter references are to *Psychology in Your Life,* Fourth High School Edition.)

1. Apply the biopsychosocial model (Figure 11.1) to some situation that worries you. Copy the cycle diagram and write down personal psychological factors, biological characteristics, and social conditions. What does your diagram reveal about the interactive nature between thoughts and actions?

2. Ample research confirms that obesity carries a stigma in our society. Check your social media for an example of "fat shaming." Describe and critique the example: What are biological factors that influence body weight? How could you respond to the post in a scientific and supportive way?

3. Section 11.3 lists the physical, emotional, and cognitive benefits of exercise. Test the Slutsky-Ganesh et al. 2020 research that exercise improves memory by working out prior to studying for an upcoming test. Was your test performance better than usual?

4. According to Shelley Taylor's research, women respond to stress differently than men. Figures 11.19 and 11.20 contrast a male's "fight or flight" response with a female's "tend and befriend" response. Share Taylor's research with an adult male and female and record their responses.

5. Figure 11.24 contrasts emotion-focused coping and problem-focused coping. Give an example of someone in your life who uses problem-focused coping and apply this coping strategy to a relevant stressor in your life.

Key Takeaways Figure 11.16 illustrates two types of stressors: major life stressors and daily hassles. Take and score the Student Stress Scale on page 444 and record daily hassles on your phone for three days. Summarize your findings and use three coping strategies to moderate your stress response.

Research in positive psychology has identified specific ways to promote resilience, hardiness, and happiness. Create a personal positive psychology plan that includes at least three research-based ideas to boost your happiness.

THE BIG QUESTION

Use research from this chapter to evaluate your own overall health (physical, emotional, and cognitive).	

Chapter 12
Social Psychology

We like to think that we are in control of our own thinking and behavior. Social psychology research casts doubt on this control: our involvement in groups and interactions with authority figures influences both our attitudes and actions. Research discussed in this chapter will help you think about how the groups you belong to may influence you, and how you influence others.

PRE-READING QUESTIONS

	ANSWER THESE QUESTIONS BEFORE you read the chapter. (You will refer to these answers again at the end of the chapter.)	REVISE YOUR ANSWERS NOW AFTER you read the chapter. Based on what you read in the chapter, revise your answer if needed.	Explain whether you predicted correctly or not, and what you know now that you didn't know before.
Humans tend to explain the behavior of others by primarily referring to situational factors.	True False		
There is a reciprocal relationship between actions and attitudes.	True False		
Performing in front of a crowd enhances performance.	True False		

RETRIEVE-AS-YOU-GO QUESTIONS

SECTION 12.1 You Tend to Make Snap Judgments About Other People

A. What is the potential value of "thin slices of behavior" mentioned in the text?

B. Is it easy or hard to detect lies based on nonverbal cues? Why?

C. Explain at least one of the research findings about facial expressions.

SECTION 12.2 You Make Attributions About Other People

A. Contrast situational and dispositional attributions.

B. Define the just world hypothesis in your own words.

C. Explain one example of the fundamental attribution error.

SECTION 12.3 You Tend to Stereotype Other People

A. Explain one example of stereotyping from the text.

B. Define "self-fulfilling prophecy" in your own words.

C. Explain one of the research findings that supports the concept of stereotype threat.

SECTION 12.4 Stereotypes Can Lead to Prejudice and Discrimination

A. Contrast prejudice and discrimination.

B. Provide one of your "ingroups" and one of your "outgroups."

C. How did Muzafer Sherif and others reduce animosity between the groups in the summer camp study?

SECTION 12.5 You Form Attitudes Through Experience and Socialization

A. What kinds of attitudes predict behavior well?

B. Define the mere exposure effect in your own words.

C. Contrast implicit and explicit attitudes.

SECTION 12.6 Discrepancies Between Attitudes and Behavior Lead to Dissonance

A. Define "cognitive dissonance" in your own words.

B. How can justification of effort explain cognitive dissonance?

SECTION 12.7 Your Attitudes Can Be Changed Through Persuasion

A. Define "persuasion" in your own words.

B. List the three factors that can affect persuasiveness.

C. Contrast the central and peripheral route to persuasion.

SECTION 12.8 Groups Affect Your Behavior

A. Contrast social facilitation and social loafing.

B. Describe an example of deindividuation.

C. What causes groupthink?

SECTION 12.9 You Conform to and Comply With Others

A. Define "conformity" in your own words.

B. Contrast normative and informational influence.

C. List some social norms that influence your behavior.

D. List the three compliance strategies mentioned in the text.

SECTION 12.10 You Probably Obey People Who Have Authority

A. What is the difference between obedience and conformity?

B. What is one of the major findings of Milgram's obedience study?

C. Explain at least one of the criticisms of Milgram's obedience study.

SECTION 12.11 You May Hurt or Help Other People

A. What are some biological influences on aggression?

B. Define the frustration-aggression hypothesis in your own words.

C. In what ways does reciprocal helping explain examples of altruism?

D. What factors influence whether bystanders will help in emergency situations?

SECTION 12.12 Situations and Personalities Affect Your Relationships

A. How do proximity and similarity influence attraction?

B. What are some physical characteristics that are considered attractive in all cultures?

C. According to research cited in the text, what is one benefit of being physically attractive?

A. Contrast companionate and passionate love.	
B. Describe how romantic relationships typically change over time.	
C. Describe the role accommodation plays in successful long-term relationships.	

Using Psychology in Your Life: Consider an option that is personally relevant. (Page and chapter references are to *Psychology in Your Life*, Fourth High School Edition.)

1. Read and analyze an article about a present-day problem from your social media newsfeed. Highlight the author's attributions, identifying examples of bias in attribution like the fundamental attribution error and the actor/observer bias (Learning Tip, p. 469). Did you find the article persuasive? Why or why not?

2. Figure 12.5 illustrates how stereotype threat can negatively impact student performance. Walton and Spencer's research shows that this impact can be reduced if exams are presented as "nonevaluative" (p. 471). Have you ever experienced or witnessed stereotype threat? What recommendation would you share with teachers to reduce stereotype threat in their classroom?

3. An older friend calls to share the exciting news that they plan to join a fraternity. What should they know about cognitive dissonance and justification of effort to prevent potentially harmful group behaviors like hazing?

4. A friend who is moving asks for your help to sell an old bicycle and sporting equipment. How can you use the three ways of inducing compliance (Table 12.1) to help them sell their stuff?

5. Describe a fashion trend, social norm, or popular tradition in your high school. Explain student behavior using the terms "normative influence" and/or "social influence."

Key Takeaways Reflect on how your thoughts, feelings, and actions are influenced by other people. Are your attitudes influenced more by socialization from family or a desire to belong with friends? What situations (school, home, work, extracurricular activities) bring out your best self? What situations make it harder for you to live according to your values?

Imagine that your principal asks your advice about how to reduce the negative impact of stereotyping, prejudice, and discrimination for students at your school, especially those in groups labeled as "out-groups." Design a proposal with at least three research-based recommendations to ensure that all students can thrive in your school.

THE BIG QUESTION

How do social groups influence your thinking and behavior?

Chapter 13
Self and Personality

Are you introverted? Extroverted? Confident? Agreeable? In this chapter, you'll learn how psychological researchers described personality over the years and attempts to measure personality traits. You'll also read about how biological and situational factors may influence your personality.

PRE-READING QUESTIONS

	ANSWER THESE QUESTIONS BEFORE you read the chapter. (You will refer to these answers again at the end of the chapter.)	REVISE YOUR ANSWERS NOW AFTER you read the chapter. Based on what you read in the chapter, revise your answer if needed.	Explain whether you predicted correctly or not, and what you know now that you didn't know before.
Culture influences many psychological traits, but personality traits are genetic, not situational.	True False		
Personality psychologists agree on the basic components of our self: the id, ego, and super ego.	True False		
Trait theory personality tests are the most well researched and accepted ways to measure personality.	True False		

RETRIEVE-AS-YOU-GO QUESTIONS

SECTION 13.1 Your Self-Concept Is What You Know and Believe About Yourself

A. Define "personality" in your own words.

B. What is the function of your self-schema?

C. Contrast self-concept and working self-concept.

SECTION 13.2 People Differ in How They Value Themselves

A. Define "self-esteem" in your own words.

B. How do self-esteem levels generally change over the life-span?

C. How does self-esteem relate to life outcomes?

D. What is the dark triad?

SECTION 13.3 You Try to Create a Positive Sense of Self

A. Define "positive illusions" in your own words.

B. Contrast downward comparisons, upward comparisons, and temporal comparisons.

C. Explain an example of self-serving bias.

SECTION 13.4 Your Sense of Self Is Influenced by Cultural Factors

A. Describe a few characteristics of an individualist culture.	
B. Describe a few characteristics of a collectivist culture.	

SECTION 13.5 Psychodynamic Theory Emphasizes Unconscious Conflicts

A. Explain the central idea of psychodynamic theory.	
B. Use the iceberg metaphor to discuss the id, ego, and superego.	
C. Why did Freud think people used defense mechanisms?	

SECTION 13.6 Humanistic Approaches Emphasize Goodness in People

A. Summarize the humanistic approach to personality.	
B. How do therapists practice person-centered therapy?	
C. What is the relationship between conditions of worth and unconditional positive regard?	

SECTION 13.7 Social Cognitive Approaches Focus on How Thoughts Shape Personality

A. How does expectancy theory explain our behaviors?	

B. Contrast internal and external locus of control.

C. Summarize reciprocal determinism in your own words.

SECTION 13.8 Trait Approaches Describe Characteristics

A. Describe the trait approach to personality research.

B. List the traits in the five factor trait theory.

C. Which of the traits in the five factor trait theory do you think are your "strongest" personality traits?

SECTION 13.9 Do Personalities Matter in Roommate Relationships?

A. What is the relationship between roommates' personality traits and relationship satisfaction?

B. What lessons can you learn from this research if you ever get to choose a roommate?

SECTION 13.10 Personality Has a Biological Basis

A. What role might the reticular activation system play in personality?

B. Explain how arousal theory might relate to introversion/extraversion.

SECTION 13.11 Personality Is Influenced by Genes

A. Why are twin studies important in personality
   research?

B. Explain the results of one of the adoption personality
   studies discussed in the text.

SECTION 13.12 Temperament Is Innate

A. Define "temperament" in your own words.

B. What are the three aspects of temperament?

C. List the temperaments described in the text, and
   explain which temperament seems to be the most
   advantageous.

SECTION 13.13 Personality Stability Is Influenced by Biology and Situation

A. How much do personality traits change or stay the
   same over our life span?

B. Contrast basic tendencies and characteristic
   adaptations.

C. Explain an example of a life situation causing
   personality change.

SECTION 13.14 Several Methods Are Used to Assess Personality

A. How do projective tests try to measure personality?

B. Why are most personality tests self-report measures?	
C. Explain how some personality researchers use technology (like smartphones) as measures of personality.	
D. How accurate are people's self-judgments compared to the way their friends describe them?	

SECTION 13.15 Behavior Is Influenced by Personality and Situation

A. Describe the "person/situation debate."	
B. Contrast the influence of strong and weak situations.	

Using Psychology in Your Life: Consider an option that is personally relevant. (Page and chapter references are to *Psychology in Your Life*, Fourth High School Edition.)

1. Jot down 10 responses to the question: Who am I? A self-schema (Figure 13.2) illustrates how memories, beliefs, and generalizations relate to your overall sense of self. Diagram your 10 responses in bubbles to create a personal self-schema.

2. Recent research suggests that self-compassion is a good predictor of mental health. Describe a time when you cared for a good friend going through a difficult time listing three specific ways you supported your friend. How could you apply each act of support to yourself when you're going through a hard time?

3. Would you describe yourself as more extraverted or introverted? Describe your ideal study setting. How do your responses compare with Figure 13.17 ("Optimal Arousal Influences Personality")?

4. Evaluate Tang et al.'s 2020 research (p. 529) finding that temperament at 14 months predicts personality at 30. Ask a parent or guardian about your activity level, emotionality, and sociability at 14 months. How does their description compare with your present personality?

5. Rate yourself 1 (least)—7 (most) on the big five personality traits (openness, conscientiousness, extraversion, agreeableness, neuroticism). Ask three friends to rate you using

the same scale. Compare the responses. Which do you think is more accurate? Why? How do your results compare to Figure 13.27?

Key Takeaways Review the "Approaches to Personality" Table (Table 13.1). Which approach most effectively describes your personality? Which approach is least effective? Back up your responses with specific examples.

How can you find a compatible roommate? Use Carli and colleagues' 1991 research about personality similarity (p. 524) and Olgetree and colleagues' 2005 research about cleanliness (p. 525) to determine specific questions to ask potential roommates to help you make the best choice.

THE BIG QUESTION

Think about your personality. How would the different personality theories summarized in this chapter describe your personality?	

Chapter 14
Psychological Disorders

If you tell someone that you are studying psychology, they might assume that you are learning exclusively about the topic of this chapter. The symptoms and causes of psychological disorders is one of the most important research areas in the science of psychology, and in this chapter you will learn how clinical psychologists define, categorize, and think about psychological disorders.

PRE-READING QUESTIONS

	ANSWER THESE QUESTIONS BEFORE you read the chapter. (You will refer to these answers again at the end of the chapter.)	REVISE YOUR ANSWERS NOW AFTER you read the chapter. Based on what you read in the chapter, revise your answer if needed.	Explain whether you predicted correctly or not, and what you know now that you didn't know before.
The most important criterion used to define psychological disorders is whether a behavior is disturbing to others.	True False		
Research into psychological disorders focuses on biological, social, and environmental causes of mental illness.	True False		
As incomes rise and poverty falls worldwide, depression levels also decrease.	True False		

RETRIEVE-AS-YOU-GO QUESTIONS

SECTION 14.1 Disorders Interfere With Our Lives

A. List the most common psychological disorders in men and women.

B. What are the four criteria clinical psychologists consider when diagnosing psychological disorders?

C. Why are clinical psychologists interested in the etiology of psychological disorders?

SECTION 14.2 There Are Two General Ways to View the Causes of Disorders

A. Explain the diathesis-stress model in your own words.

B. How does the biopsychosocial approach explain the causes of psychological disorders?

C. Summarize one of the research findings about the impact of the COVID-19 pandemic on mental health.

SECTION 14.3 Disordered Thoughts, Emotions, and Behaviors Can Be Assessed and Categorized

A. Describe some of the ways clinical psychologists gather information through assessments.

B. What is the purpose of the DSM-5?

C. Explain what a "cultural syndrome" is.

SECTION 14.4 Anxiety Disorders Make People Fearful and Tense

A. List some of the common symptoms of anxiety disorders.

B. Define "specific phobia" in your own words.

C. Contrast social anxiety disorder and generalized anxiety disorder.

D. Explain the etiology of anxiety disorders.

SECTION 14.5 Some Disorders Involve Unwanted and Intrusive Thoughts That Increase Anxiety

A. What are some common symptoms of obsessive-compulsive disorder?

B. Describe how the biopsychosocial approach explains the development of obsessive-compulsive disorder.

C. List some of the common symptoms of posttraumatic stress disorder.

SECTION 14.6 Depressive Disorders Involve Sad, Empty, or Irritable Mood

A. List some of the common symptoms of depressive disorders.

B. Contrast major depressive disorder and persistent depressive disorder.

C. Why is depression called the "common cold" of psychological disorders?

SECTION 14.7 Many Factors Influence the Development of Depressive Disorders

A. What are some of the biological factors involved in depressive disorders?

B. What are some of the psychological factors involved in depressive disorders?

C. What are some of the sociocultural factors involved in depressive disorders?

SECTION 14.8 What Should You Do If You Think a Friend or Loved One Might Be Considering Suicide?

A. What happened to the rates of suicidal ideation and suicide attempts over the last 20 years?

B. What kinds of interpersonal distress seems to be most likely related to suicide?

C. What should you do if you know someone who you think may attempt suicide? List the three pieces of advice from the text.

SECTION 14.9 Bipolar Disorders Involve Mania

A. What are common symptoms of bipolar disorder?

B. Explain one of the differences between bipolar I disorder and bipolar II disorder.

C. How common is bipolar disorder?

SECTION 14.10 Schizophrenia Involves a Disconnection From Reality

A. What are common symptoms of schizophrenia?

B. List some positive and negative symptoms of schizophrenia.

C. What is the difference between a hallucination and a delusion?

SECTION 14.11 Schizophrenia Is Caused by Biological and Environmental Factors

A. Why do researchers think that genetic inheritance is highly involved in schizophrenia?

B. What environmental factors might influence the onset of schizophrenia?

SECTION 14.12 Personality Disorders Are Maladaptive Ways of Relating to the World

A. Provide one personality disorder from each cluster described in the text.

B. Describe borderline personality disorder in your own words.

C. Describe antisocial personality disorder in your own words.

SECTION 14.13 Dissociative Disorders Involve Disruptions in the Sense of Self

A. What is the common characteristic of the dissociative disorders?

B. Describe dissociative amnesia in your own words.

C. Explain the controversy about the existence of dissociative identity disorder.

SECTION 14.14 Eating Disorders Involve Distortions or Distress About Body Image

A. Describe common symptoms of anorexia nervosa.

B. What are the similarities between bulimia nervosa and anorexia nervosa? What are the differences?

C. What is binge-eating disorder?

SECTION 14.15 Children May Experience Neurodevelopmental Disorders

A. What is one common characteristic of all the neurodevelopmental disorders?

B. Why is it important to think about neurodevelopmental disorders in the context of maturational age?

SECTION 14.16 Autism Spectrum Disorder Involves Social Deficits and Restricted Interests

A. Describe autism spectrum disorder in your own words.

B. List some typical symptoms of autism spectrum disorder.

C. What do researchers think are possible environmental risk factors for the development of autism spectrum disorder?

A. List typical symptoms of attention-deficit/hyperactivity disorder.	
B. Discuss what researchers know about the etiology of attention-deficit/hyperactivity disorder.	
C. Describe some symptoms experienced by adults with attention-deficit/hyperactivity disorder.	

Using Psychology in Your Life: Consider an option that is personally relevant. (Page and chapter references are to *Psychology in Your Life*, Fourth High School Edition.)

1. Examine Figure 14.1, "Sex Differences in Psychological Disorders." Pick a disorder that has a significant sex difference and hypothesize a possible reason for this difference. Use evidence about etiology of the disorder to support your argument.

2. Figures 14.11 and 14.18 show how distorted thoughts and perceptions can fuel symptoms of anxiety and depressive disorders. According to Aaron Beck's Cognitive Triad (p. 564), individuals with depression have negative perceptions of self, future, and situation. Apply Beck's triad to how a classmate with depression would explain getting a bad grade on a test.

3. In his book *Why People Die by Suicide*, Thomas Joiner states that "people desire death when two fundamental needs are frustrated" (p. 566). Summarize these two needs. List three specific ways that you could help a friend who you are worried might harm themself.

4. A friend is concerned that their sister might have an eating disorder because she is constantly dieting. Explain to your friend how a professional would determine if their sister suffers from anorexia nervosa.

5. Imagine that you are working in an afterschool program for sixth graders. You are told that a student in your group has autism spectrum disorder. What behaviors can you expect? How can you best help this student feel included and comfortable?

Key Takeaways The pandemic has increased mental health concerns worldwide. The biopsychosocial model (Figure 14.4) illustrates that psychological disorders are influenced by an interaction of nature and nurture. Pick one disorder described in chapter 14 and discuss the environmental and psychological causes of this disorder. Make recommendations about how to ease symptoms and reduce causes where possible.

Chapter 14 includes many case studies of celebrities who share their experience with psychological disorders in order to reduce the stigma associated with mental illness. Pick one case study to research further. Summarize your findings, including an inspirational quote. How does this celebrity's story affect your view about psychological disorders?

THE BIG QUESTION

What life experiences have you had with psychological disorders? What information from this chapter confirms or contradicts what you thought you knew about psychological disorders?

Chapter 15
Psychological Treatments

One of the most important purposes of psychological research is to help people who are experiencing symptoms of psychological disorders. If you haven't needed help from a clinical psychologist yet in your life, it is quite possible that you will someday. It's even more likely that someone you love benefits from psychotherapy. In this chapter you will learn about clinical psychological therapies, and ways to find safe and effective treatments.

PRE-READING QUESTIONS

	ANSWER THESE QUESTIONS BEFORE you read the chapter. (You will refer to these answers again at the end of the chapter.)	REVISE YOUR ANSWERS NOW AFTER you read the chapter. Based on what you read in the chapter, revise your answer if needed.	Explain whether you predicted correctly or not, and what you know now that you didn't know before.
Modern clinical psychologists focus on biomedical therapies rather than outdated "talk therapies."	True False		
Therapies can't be truly evaluated with traditional experimental research methods.	True False		
Operant and classical conditioning techniques are important components of some therapies.	True False		

RETRIEVE-AS-YOU-GO QUESTIONS

SECTION 15.1 Some Types of Psychotherapy Focus on Providing Insight

A. Define "psychotherapy" in your own words.

B. What methods do psychodynamic therapists use to help clients?

C. In what ways do psychodynamic therapists use some of Freud's ideas?

D. Summarize humanistic therapy in your own words.

SECTION 15.2 Behavioral and Cognitive Treatments Aim to Change Thoughts, Feelings, and Behaviors Directly

A. What is the main idea behind behavioral therapy?

B. Summarize cognitive therapy in your own words.

C. Describe an example of cognitive-behavioral therapy.

SECTION 15.3 The Context of Therapy Matters

A. Explain one of the advantages of group therapy.

B. Explain how the systems approach relates to family therapy.

C. How do cultural beliefs impact treatment?

SECTION 15.4 Biological Therapies Are Effective for Certain Disorders

A. List the five categories of psychotropic medications.

B. What kind of psychotropic drugs are SSRIs? What does SSRI mean?

C. Compare ECT and TMS as therapeutic techniques.

SECTION 15.5 Scientific Evidence Indicates Which Treatments Are Safe and Effective

A. What is the most accurate way to research the effectiveness of different kinds of therapies?

B. What are the three features that characterize evidence-based psychological treatments?

SECTION 15.6 Various Providers Assist in Treating Psychological Disorders

A. What is one of the important differences between clinical psychologists and psychiatrists?

B. Which kinds of psychological issues seem to be effectively treated with technology based treatments (like specialized cell phone apps)?

SECTION 15.7 How Do You Find a Provider Who Can Help You?

A. What advice does the text offer about determining if you need therapy?

B. What kinds of issues can therapists help with?

C. How can you determine whether a therapist is a good match for your needs?

SECTION 15.8 Anxiety and Obsessive-Compulsive Disorders Are Best Treated With Cognitive Behavioral Therapy

A. Explain the exposure component of CBT therapy.

B. Explain how classical conditioning can be useful during the treatment of anxiety disorders.

C. Describe systematic desensitization in your own words.

D. What is the most common treatment for OCD?

SECTION 15.9 Many Effective Treatments Are Available for Depressive Disorders

A. Explain how SSRIs may be helpful with depression.

B. Describe how CBT is used to treat depression.

C. What are some alternative treatments for depression?

SECTION 15.10 Psychotropic Medications Are Most Effective for Bipolar Disorders

A. What kinds of drugs are used to treat bipolar disorders?

B. Explain an advantage of SSRIs over other drugs in the treatment of bipolar disorder.

SECTION 15.11 Atypical Antipsychotic Medications Are the Best Treatment for Schizophrenia

A. What medications are often used to treat schizophrenia symptoms?	
B. Explain some of the advantages of atypical antipsychotic medications.	
C. How can behavior therapies be helpful for people suffering from schizophrenia?	

SECTION 15.12 Dialectical Behavior Therapy Is the Best Treatment for Borderline Personality Disorder

A. Explain dialectical behavior therapy in your own words.	
B. How effective is dialectical behavior therapy in the treatment of borderline personality disorder?	

SECTION 15.13 Antisocial Personality Disorder Is Extremely Difficult to Treat

A. Why is antisocial personality disorder difficult to treat?	
B. How do therapists use operant procedures in the treatment of antisocial personality disorder?	
C. How effective is antisocial personality disorder treatment long term?	

SECTION 15.14 Children With Autism Spectrum Disorder Benefit From Structured Behavior Therapy

A. Explain applied behavioral analysis in your own words.	
B. Explain naturalistic developmental behavioral interventions in your own words.	

A. What is the most common medical treatment for ADHD?	
B. How is behavior therapy sometimes useful during ADHD treatment?	

Using Psychology in Your Life: Consider an option that is personally relevant. (Page and chapter references are to *Psychology in Your Life*, Fourth High School Edition.)

1. Describe a person in your life who shows you unconditional positive regard. How does this person compare to a humanistic therapist? In what ways are they similar? Different?

2. A friend of yours blames themself for a recent and painful breakup. Use cognitive restructuring techniques (Figure 15.5) to help your friend reduce depressed feelings and increase positive thoughts. Include ways that you would correct specific statements your friend might make.

3. A friend has aerophobia and is terrified about an upcoming flight to a family occasion. Create an anxiety hierarchy for fear of flying (Table 15.5), and explain how you would use systematic desensitization to help them reduce their fear.

4. Depression is widespread, particularly for adolescents. In order to educate classmates, create a one-page handout or infographic summarizing best treatments for depression.

5. Your friend, recently diagnosed with ADHD and prescribed Ritalin, is concerned about becoming dependent on the medication. Explain how the medication works to improve academic performance. How could behavioral therapy be used to supplement medication to ultimately phase out reliance on Ritalin?

Key Takeaways There are many careers that help people struggling with mental health issues. Review Table 15.3 (Providers of Psychological Treatment), particularly the "employment" column. What roles and settings appeal to you? Why? What roles and settings do not appeal to you? Why?

Given that nearly half of all Americans meet the criteria for a psychological disorder sometime in their life (p. 604), finding the right therapist is important both for self-care and caring for loved ones. Summarize the textbook's advice in "How Do You Find a Provider Who Can Help You?" (Section 15.7) in words that someone with no familiarity with psychology would understand. What do you think is the most important information to share?

THE BIG QUESTION

What did you learn in this chapter that you would use if someone you love told you they thought they needed some help from a clinical psychologist?